COMPOSER
SHOWCASE
HAL LEONARD
STUDENT PIANO LIBRARY

County Ragtime Festival

SEVEN ORIGINAL RAGS FOR PIANO SOLO

BY FRED KERN

CONTENTS

ISBN 978-1-4584-1396-3

HAL•LEONARD®
CORPORATION
7777 W. BLUEMOUND RD. P.O. BOX 13819 MILWAUKEE, WI 53213

In Australia Contact:
Hal Leonard Australia Pty. Ltd.
4 Lentara Court
Cheltenham, Victoria, 3192 Australia
Email: ausadmin@halleonard.com.au

Visit Hal Leonard Online at
www.halleonard.com

County Fair Rag

Fred Kern

Spirited (♩ = 120)

Both hands 8va 2nd time

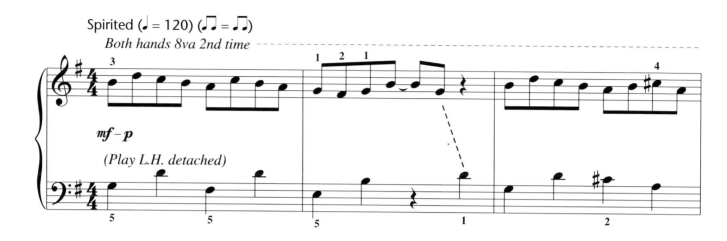

mf – p

(Play L.H. detached)

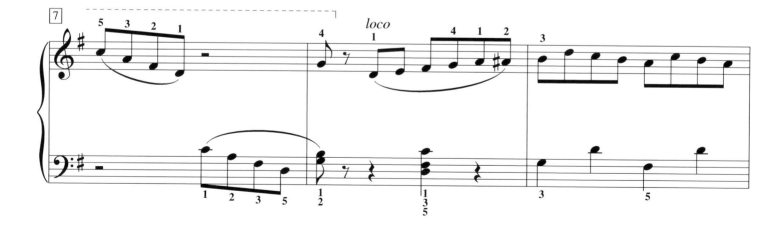

loco

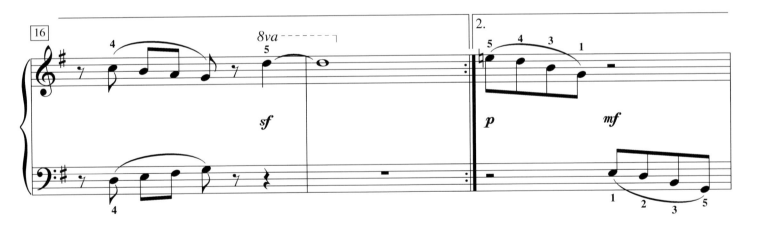

Courthouse Rag
("The Red Dome")

Fred Kern

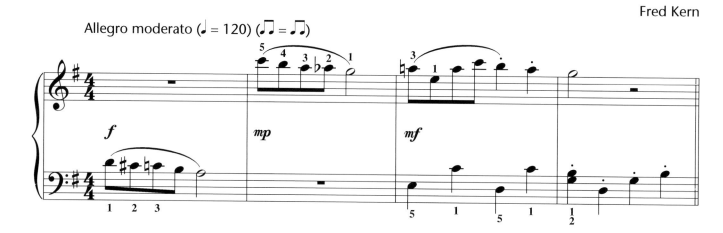

To Coda ⊕

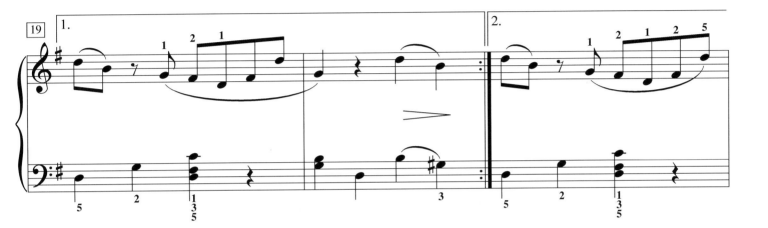

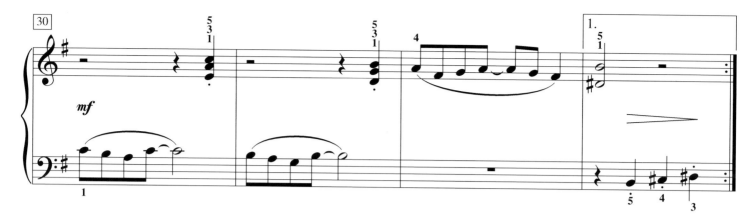

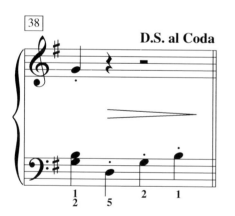

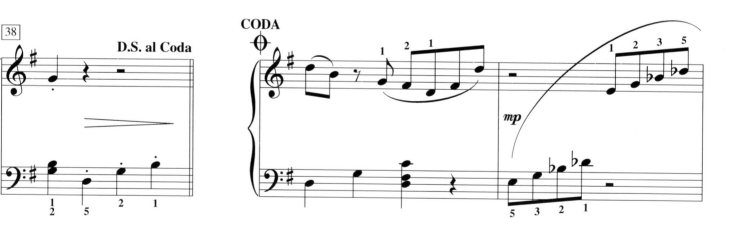

In Fields of Green
(Ragtime Waltz)

Fred Kern

Slow Waltz (♩ = 80)

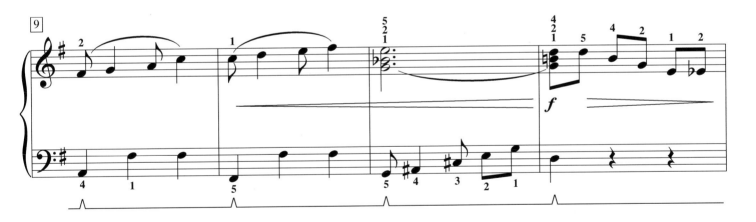

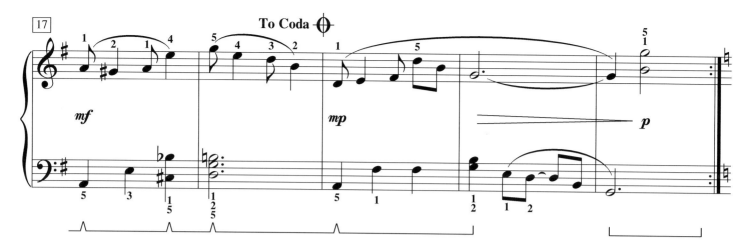

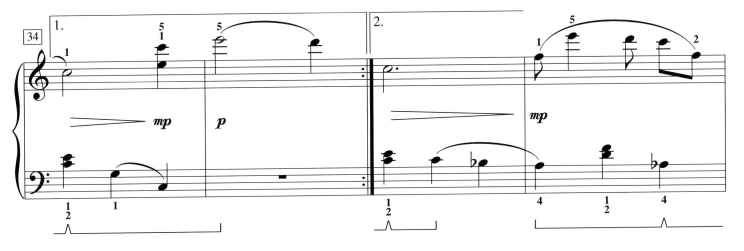

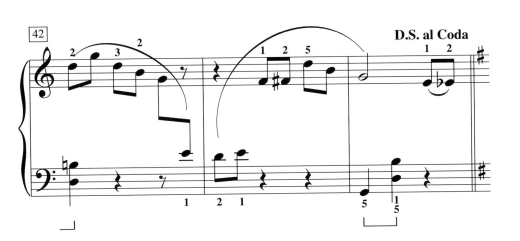
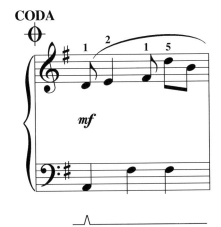

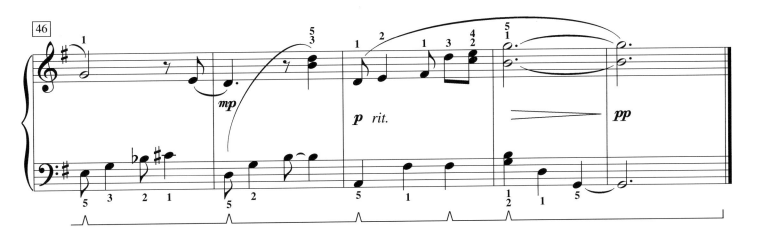

Easy Does It

Fred Kern

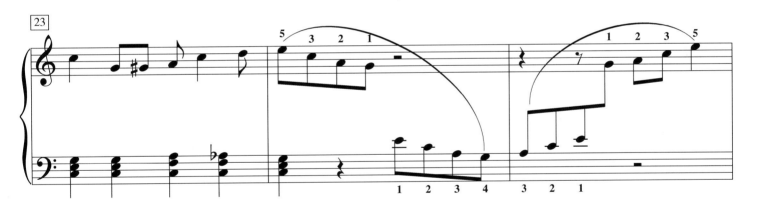

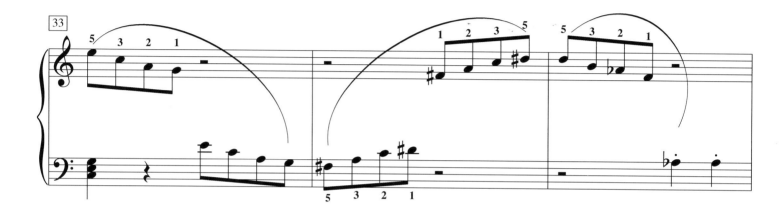

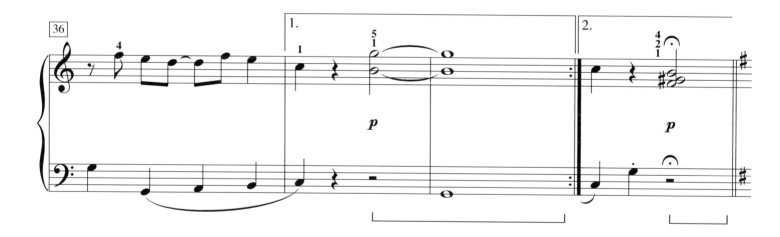

Honey Creek Rag

Fred Kern

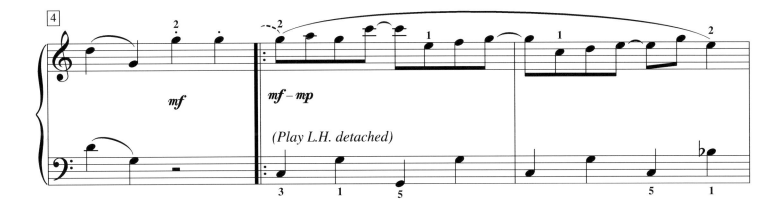

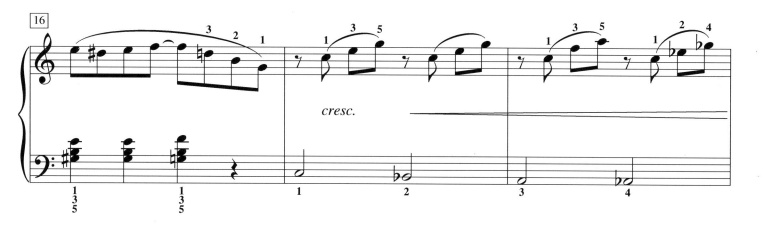

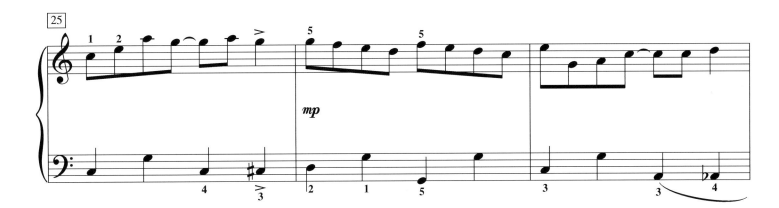

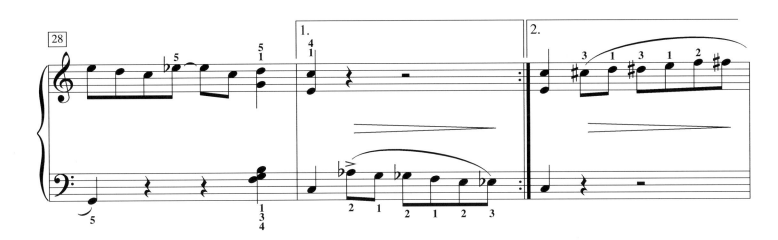

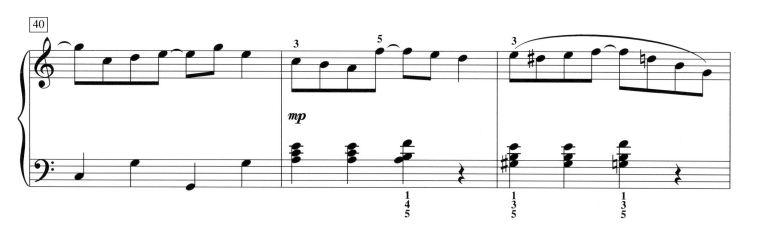

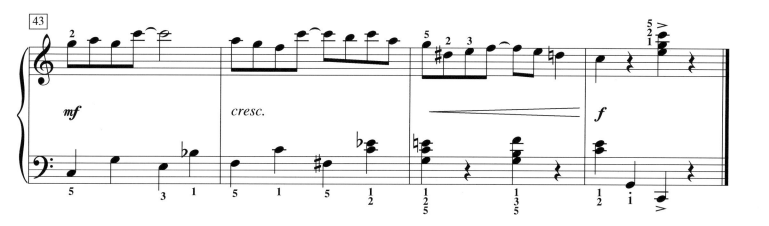

Prairie School Rag

Fred Kern

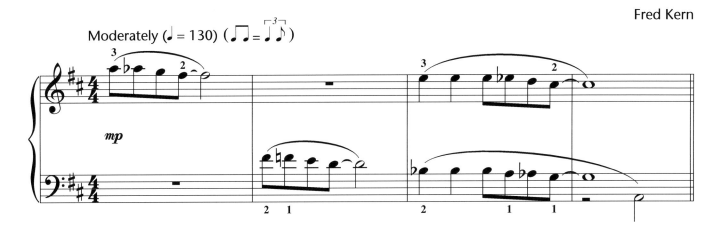

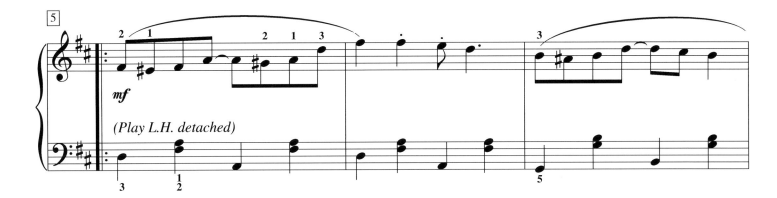

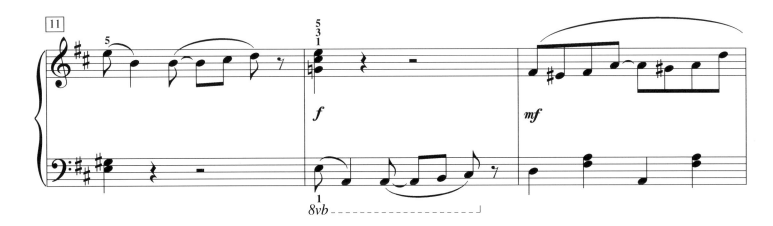

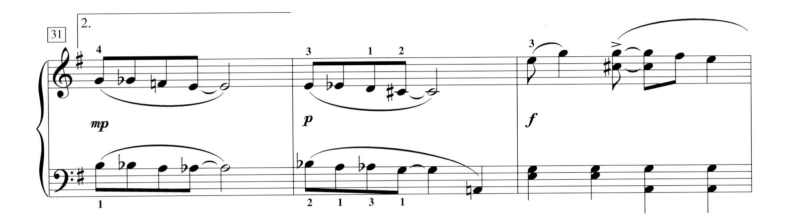

Party Line Rag

Fred Kern

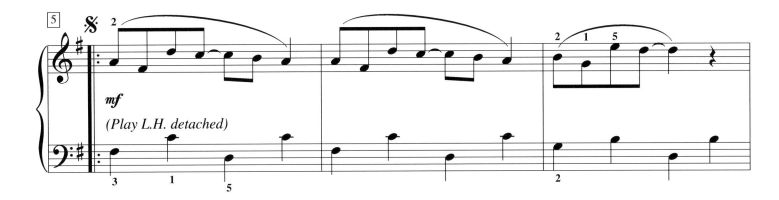

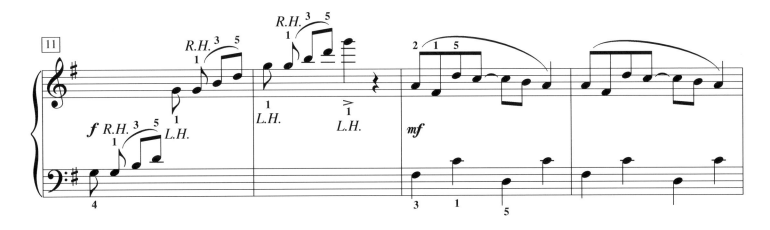

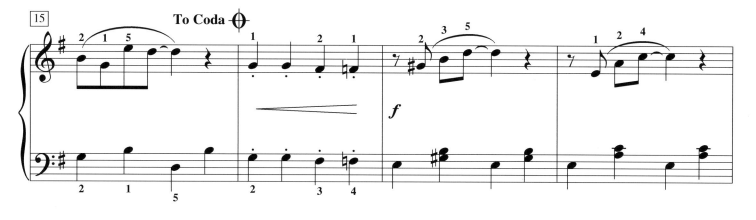

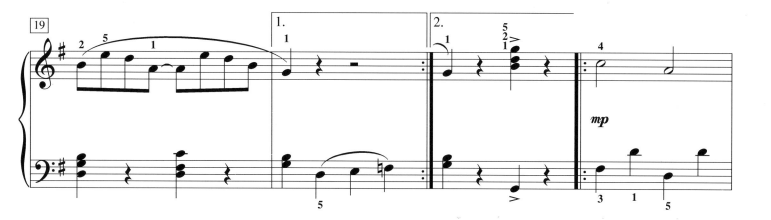

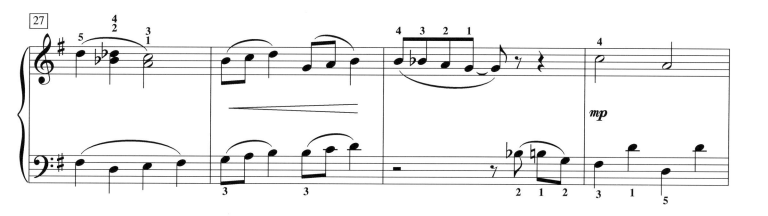